Potty Training Made Easy

Dr. Baruch Kushnir

APP

The app turns the book's text into catchy songs your kids are sure to enjoy! Download the app and add another dimension to the toilet training process.

The Magic Bowl
Potty training Made Easy

Dr. Baruch Kushnir

Professional content and production: Dr. Baruch Kushnir
Illustrations: Anat Zverdling
Script: Geula Grossman
Graphic design: Simone Menachem
Digital Media Processing: Nimrod Ben Zur – Nimitz TV

www.bedwettingexpert.com

info@bedwettingexpert.com

ISBN 978-965-92864-4-7

To my grandchildren

We are
Sammy Joe's parents

I am the
magic bowl

I am
Sammy Joe
King of the underworld

I am the **Diaper**

I am **Cindy**
A real bathroom champ

We are
Jennifer's Parents

I am **Jennifer**.
I do not need diapers
any more.

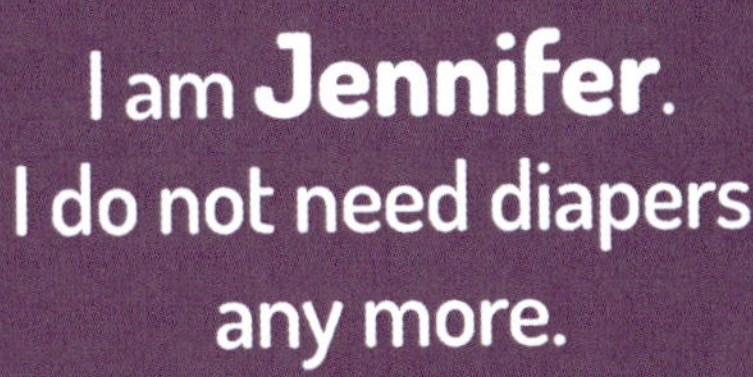

Who will teach us how to wipe?

Who will stick stickers inside the toilet bowl?

What shirt will fit Cindy at the boutique?

Who will be a bathroom champ?

Who will not see the hippo at the Zoo?

What will Jennifer do in the middle of the game?

Who lives on Crab Apple Row?

What will happen in the car?

What song will help the poo to come out?

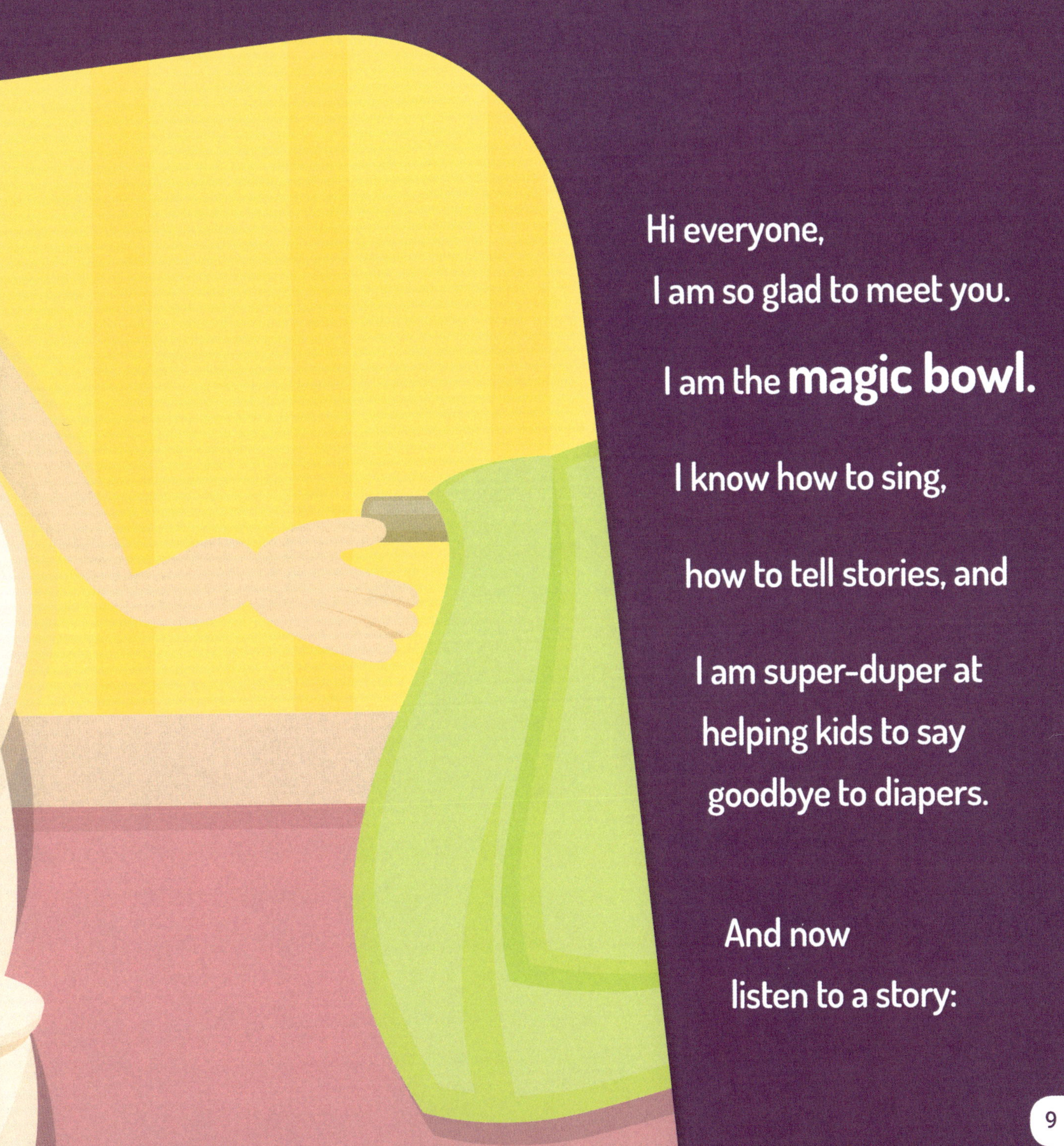

Hi everyone,

I am so glad to meet you.

I am the **magic bowl.**

I know how to sing,

how to tell stories, and

I am super-duper at

helping kids to say

goodbye to diapers.

And now

listen to a story:

Jennifer, Cindy, and Sammy Joe
Live near
each other on
Crab Apple Row.

They know how to sit.

They've learned how
to crawl,

To play in the sand and
run after a ball.

They walk and they
clap and they eat with
a spoon

And fingerpaint
all afternoon.

They dress and undress as they like and with ease

And pull up their hats as fast as they please.

Together they skip to school down the road

But they still have to wear...

their

diapers

all day.

And then...
one day,

it all started...

Day 1

During the afternoon, in the middle of the game...

"What's THAT, Jennifer? What are you wearing?" asked Sammy Joe.

"Where is your diaper?" added Cindy.

"I don't wear diapers anymore.

These are panties.

I make peepee and poopy only in the toilet.

Look!
I'm a Bathroom
Champ now.

Wait a minute.
I gotta go to
the bathroom."

I was so excited
and started to sing:

Jennifer knows how to stay nice and clean. She climbs on the toilet and sits like a queen. She flushes the toilet and pulls up her pants. She goes to the sink and she washes her hands.

"Wow, look at that **shiny medal**," said Sammy Joe.

"We've been waiting for you," said Cindy.

"But I have a nice diaper. I have it all the time,"

said Sammy Joe.

"Yes, I really AM nice.
With me you can
keep playing forever
and ever,"

answered the diaper.

"But what if
you get wet?"

asked Cindy
and Jennifer.

"Umm...,
that doesn't
feel so good."

"What's the problem?
I don't get it!
You take another
diaper, a clean one,
and Mom will
change you."

"It's not nice to pee
when I'm in
the middle of
a sentence!"

cried the diaper.

"But Mommy
isn't here!
I'm wet,
and I wanna
keep playing."

And then I started to sing:

When you feel the diaper is itchy, wet, and thick,
It's time to try the toilet by the sink...

Day 2

What a great day.
Dad and Sammy Joe
visit the Zoo.

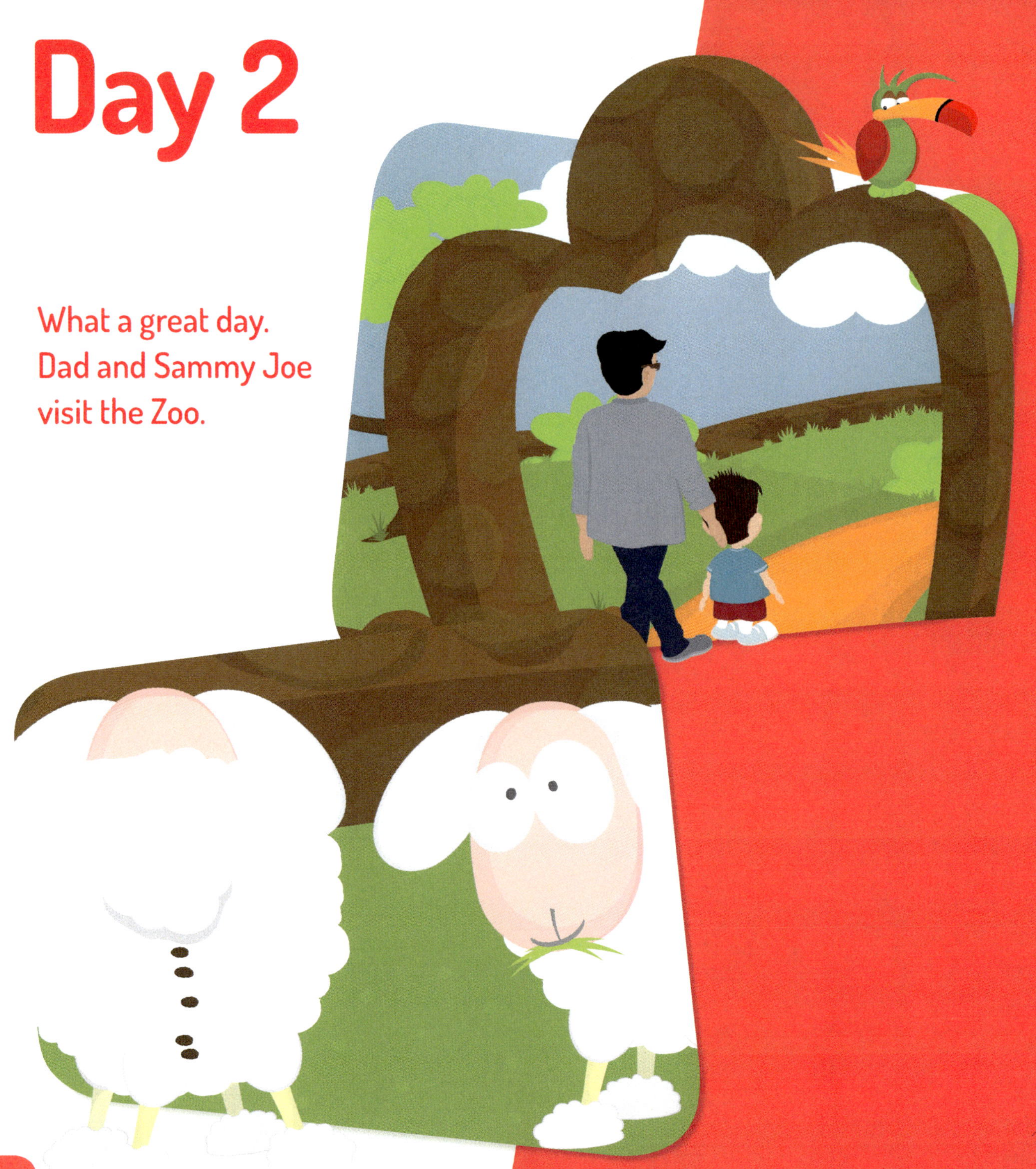

Just before the hippo,
Dad said,

"Sammy Joe, let's
stop for a minute.
**I need to go the
bathroom."**

Sammy Joe stared and thought to himself,

"I also want to stand like everyone else

and pee into this sink. It's not hard at all."

All of a sudden...

"Hey, hey, Sammy Joe, what a flood. It's awfully wet in here,"

panicked the diaper.

"Dad, I need a new diaper."

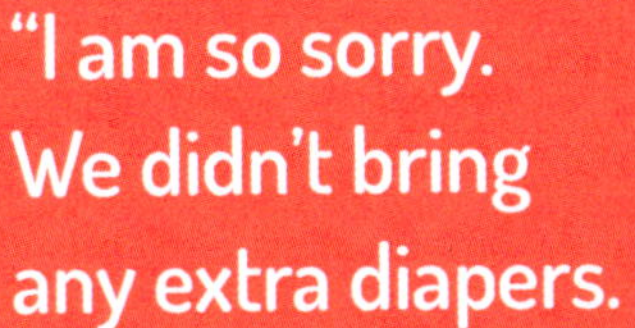

"I am so sorry. We didn't bring any extra diapers.

We're gonna have to go home."

"But Daddy, we didn't see the hippo yet."

They had no choice. Dad and Sammy Joe returned home disappointed.

"A monkey sat on an elephant's back, strolling along on a jungle track. Who did they see coming down the road? A friendly hippo and a toad."

"What a shame
we didn't see the
hippo today.

We were rushing
to change
my diaper."

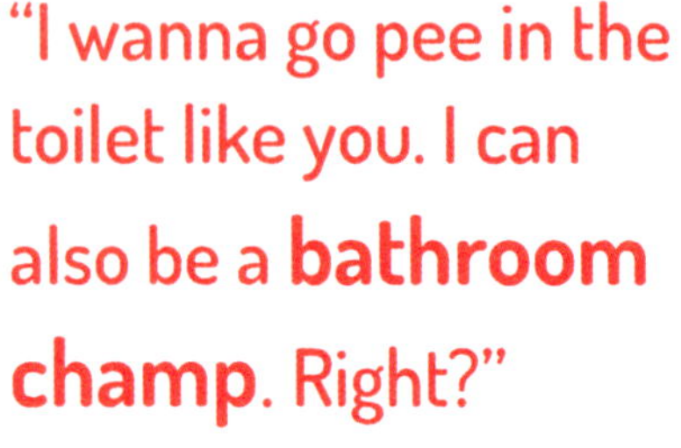

"I wanna go pee in the toilet like you. I can also be a **bathroom champ**. Right?"

"Sure. Great idea.

Let's start in the morning."

And I started to whisper:

When you feel the diaper is icky, wet, and thick
It's time to have a try at the toilet by the sink.

Day 3

Good morning,
my friends.
Shall we start?

“But the toilet is so high. There is no way I can reach it.”

“This footstool
will help.

Here. Try it.”

When Dad saw Sammy Joe so embarrassed and disappointed, he encouraged him and said,

"Let's play the Sticker Game.

You need to aim and hit the sticker."

Sammy Joe tried again and again, and I sang to encourage him,

You need to try,
you need to aim,
It's so much fun to play
this game.

Practice always pays, you see. Hit the target, perfectly.

Guess what happened
in the end?

Sammy Joe aimed
and hit the sticker.

Day 4

What a great day.
Mom and Cindy are
having fun at the mall.

Cindy tried a skirt,
shorts, and a dress.
Nothing fitted.

Something was in the way.

"Oh, look!
It's popping up."

"And here, it's way too puffy."

"And this one is poking out."

"Now it looks too full."

"Mom, enough. **The diaper** **is annoying!"**

Nothing fitted.

Mom and Cindy returned home.

Before bedtime Cindy looked at the mirior and imagined herself wearing beautiful panties and a magnificent dress.

And then she realized **she still had a diaper.**

And I started to sing,

When you feel
the diaper is icky,
wet, and thick,

It's time to have a try
at the toilet by the sink.

"Excuse me!
Am I icky?"
asked the diaper.

Instead of answering him
Cindy said,

"Mom, I also want
beautiful panties like
Jennifer."

"And you'll manage
without a diaper?"

asked Mom.

"No. No way."

"Sure. You bet."

“Excellent,” said Mom.

“Let’s start tomorrow.”

Day 5

In the morning Mom, Dad, and Cindy entered the bathroom.

Cindy looked inside and said,

"Woww...it is so deep!"

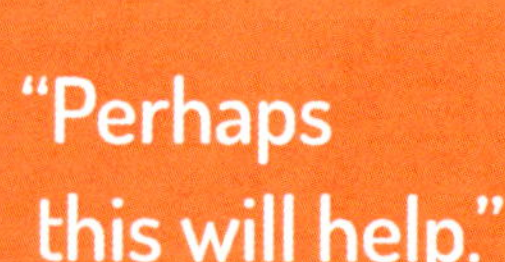

"Perhaps this will help."

"Hey,
a potty seat!"
said Cindy.

And I started to sing,

Don't be afraid.
It's just like a chair.
I'll give you a hand and
you're already there.
You can climb higher.
It's easily done. Come,
my sweetie, you'll see
that it's fun.

Cindy was very excited.

She climbed and sat down.

"And here's something else for you."

"Woo-hoo!
Thanks, Mom."

And this is from me,
bathroom champ.

Day 6

Jeniffer, Cindy,
and Sammy Joe,

super cool kids
from Crab Apple Row.

Theyr'e all through
with diapers.

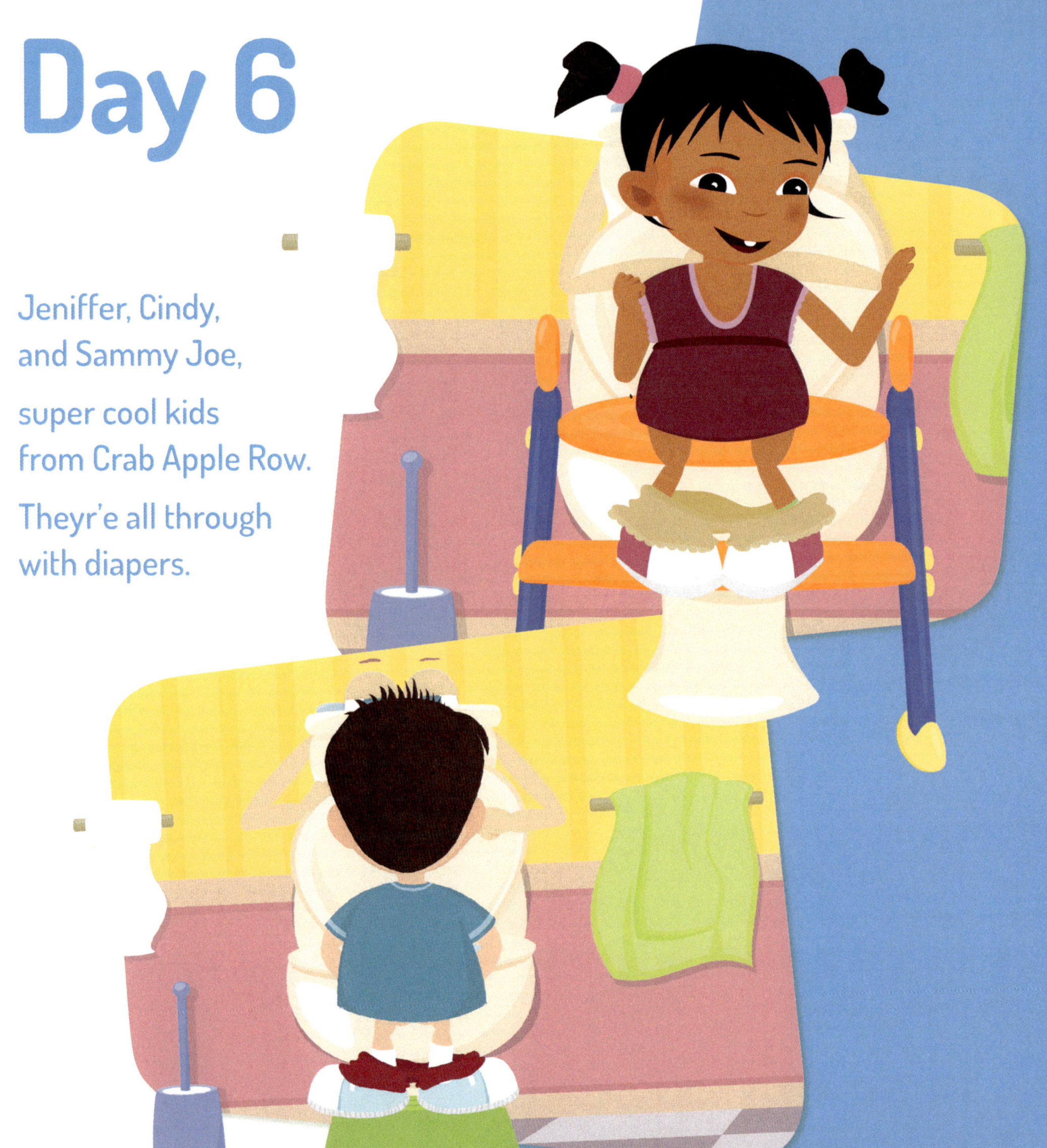

But it happens to girls. It happens to boys. It can happen to anyone once in a while.

Sometime you forget. Your head is in a cloud, and then by mistake the peepee runs out.

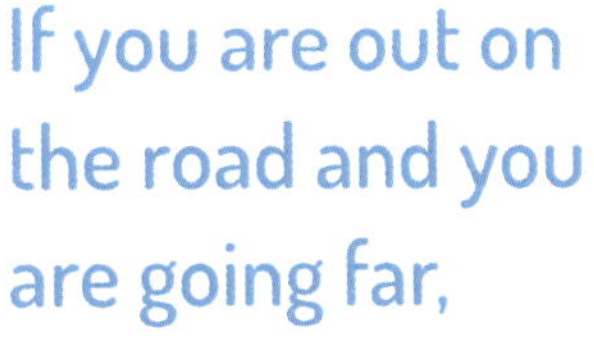

If you are out on the road and you are going far,

It can suddenly happen right in the car.

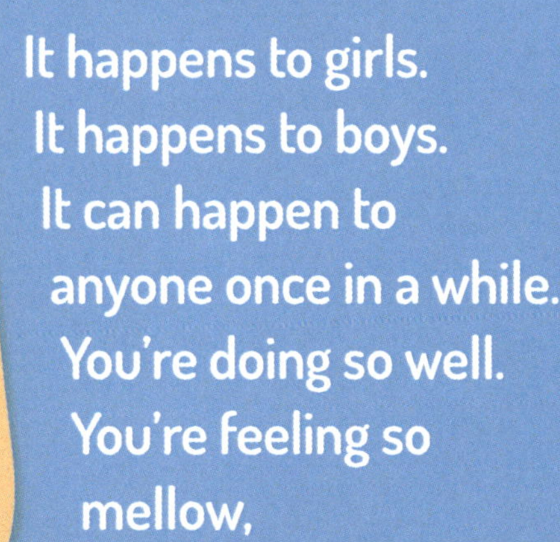

It happens to girls.
It happens to boys.
It can happen to anyone once in a while.
You're doing so well.
You're feeling so mellow,

but when you get up... Oh dear! More yellow!

Fewer clothes on the clothesline every day.

No more mess.

When you try and hold every drop, very soon the accidents will stop.

Day 7

You really are trying as hard as you can, but sometimes your bum just can't stick to the plan. You rush to the toilet, you sit and wait, and the poopy just won't cooperate.

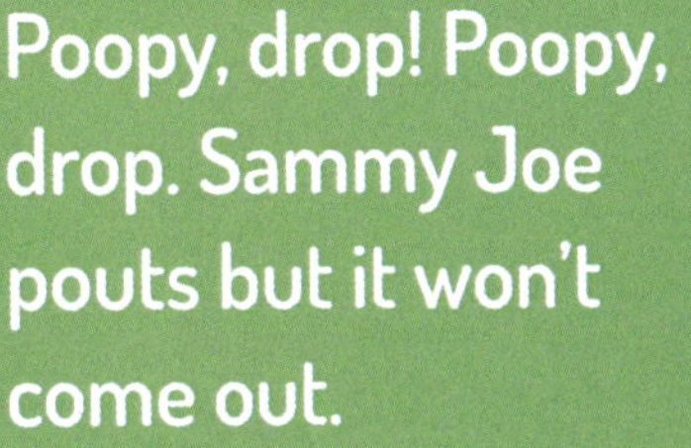

Poopy, drop! Poopy, drop. Sammy Joe pouts but it won't come out.

The clock ticks and tocks. The clock ticks loud. But nothing, nothing at all comes out.

Oof, there is nothing here.
The toilet is empty.
I'll be here until
I'm twenty.
Poopy, drop!
Poopy, drop!
Ooh, it's still not
coming out.

"That's okay,
Sammy Joe.
Sometimes
there is nothing
but sometimes..."

"I know.
You've got to go."

Sammy Joe returned to his friends.

Suddenly he stopped the game and said, "I think I have to go," and he rushed back home.

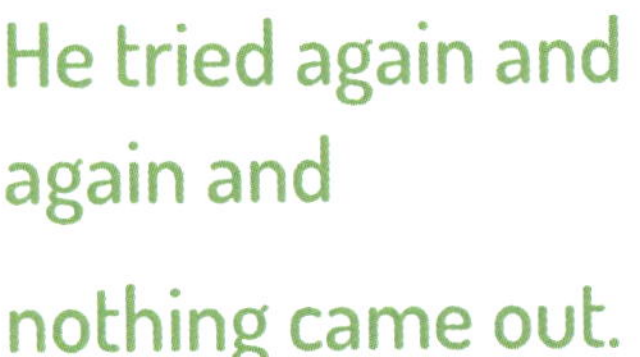

He tried again and
again and
nothing came out.

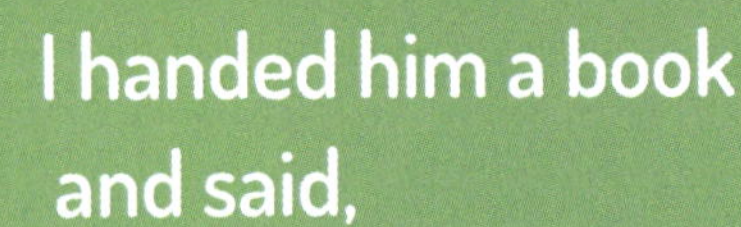

I handed him a book
and said,
Why not look
at some pictures
until the poopy
slides out.

We kept singing:

Poopy, drop!

Poopy, drop!

And then we heard the **"plop."**

It came out at last.

Day 8

In the morning
the diaper bursted in
the bathroom.

Hello Mister diaper,
how are you this
morning?

"You really want
to know?
Awful, terrible, lousy.

I used to think I was
great. I have to set
them straight.

I absolutely don't
deserve this fate.

Just look here
and next door:

kids aged two to four.

They have no use
for diapers anymore."

Hey, Mr. D. It's time to say goodbye.

Everybody knows that big kids like dry clothes.

And diapers are for baby girls and boys!

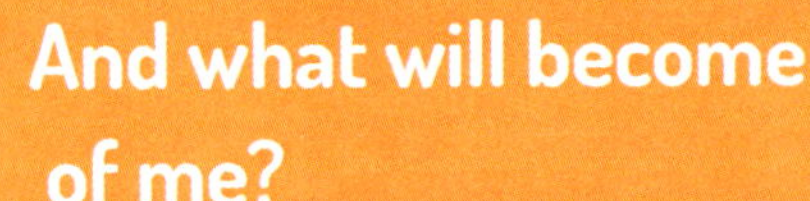

And what will become of me?

No one seems to care. The toilet is the dummest kind of chair.

I am charming debonair.

There is really nothing that's more handsome to wear.

Dearest Mr. D.,
everything will be OK.

A cute new baby is
born every single day.

"Okay, I got it.
I am going now.
Bye, everyone!"

Welcome, welcome!

The three bathroom champs

have come for a visit.

Everyone here got excited.

The toilet paper, the soap box, and even the toothbrush.

Everyone cheered,

"Hooray, hooray! The new bathroom champs."

"I've been making peepee and poopy in the toilet for weeks."

"Me too! I have new panties."

That was a great party.

Everyone started to sing and dance.

Hooray, hooray!

Let's all sing hooray
for three bathroom
champs that we are
proud of today.

They know how to stay
dry and clean with a
simple bathroom routine.

We wipe with paper
that hangs on the wall.

This is the seat where
I sit proud and tall.

Pull the handle.

You'll do fine flushing water down to make the toilet shine.

When we are finished, we're feeling great.

In the sink, we wash our hands.

We tidy up.

We're neat and dry.

Now it's time to say goodbye.

Well, kids. We have come to the end of our story, and
you can also become bathroom champs.
Just like Jennifer, Cindy, and Sammy Joe.

If you enjoyed my book, please leave a review to let others know that they, too, can benefit from this book.

Your reviews will also help me see what is and isn't working so I can better serve all my readers.

Regards,
Dr. Baruch Kushnir

Review

Made in the USA
Monee, IL
12 June 2021

71059454R00045